Be Still, Gill and Bill!

By Sascha Goddard

Bill was sad.

His pal Gill will not get up.

Gill was not ill.

Gill hid.

I will sit in my shell.

"Will we swim up top, Gill?"
said Bill.

No! I can see Nell the big gull.
Be still! Be stiff!

But Bill did not see Nell.

"Look up, Bill!
It's Nell's legs!" yells Gill.
"Nell will get us with her bill!"

"Bill, get in my shell!"
yells Gill.

Gill and Bill hid.

Gill, I am glad we are pals.

"Where is Nell, Gill?"
said Bill.

"I can not see her!" said Gill.

"We can swim up top, Gill!" said Bill.

"Let's have fun!" said Gill.

CHECKING FOR MEANING

1. Why is Bill sad? *(Literal)*

2. Why were Gill and Bill afraid of Nell? *(Literal)*

3. Why did Gill and Bill need to be still and stiff? *(Inferential)*

EXTENDING VOCABULARY

ill	What does it mean to be *ill*? What are other words that have a similar meaning? E.g. sick, unwell.
gull	What is a *gull*? What are the names of other birds you know? E.g. parrot, magpie, cockatoo. What do these birds look like?
still	What does *still* mean? What are other words we can use to mean *still*? E.g. not moving, resting.

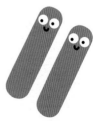

MOVING BEYOND THE TEXT

1. Where do gulls live?

2. What do gulls eat? How do they catch their food?

3. How can fish stay safe from gulls or other birds?

4. What are other animals you know that eat fish?

SPEED SOUNDS

ff	ll	ss	zz

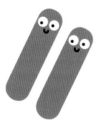

PRACTICE WORDS

Bill

Gill

will

ill

shell

Will

gull

yells

Nell

still

stiff

bill